"Never underestimate the power
you have to take your life
in a new direction"

-Germany Kent

Standing In Our GREATNESS

SELF-LOVE

By Certified Life Coach and Children's Author Reea Rodney

SELF-LOVE WORKBOOK

Copyright © 2017 Dara Wisdom and Empowerment Coaching / Reea Rodney

All rights reserved. This book or any part of it, may not be reproduced, in any form without written permission.

Printed in the United States of America
ISBN: 978-0-9975059-9-3

Written by Reea Rodney
Illustrated by Alexandra Gold
Designed by FindlayCreative.com

Standing In Our Greatness
Improving Your Self-Love Workshop

Table of Contents

Page 4	Introduction
Page 5	About the Author
Page 6	What is Self-Love
Page 7	Why is it Important to Practice Self-Love?
Page 8	Positive Impact of Self-Love
Page 9	Fun Ways To Promote Self-Love at Home and School
Page 10	Parents Tips for Promoting Self-Love
Page 11	More Parents Tips for Promoting Self-Love
	Self-Love Activities:
Page 12	Activity 1 – Daily Self-Love Worksheet
Page 13	Activity 2 – Support System
Page 14	Activity 3 – I know Who I Am
Page 15	Activity 4 – Positive Self-Talk Flower
Page 16	Activity 5 – 50 Things I love
Page 17	Activity 6 – Making Choices
Page 18	Activity 7 – My Gratitude List
Page 19	Activity 8 – My "I Love Jar"
Page 20	Activity 9 – Let's get physical
Page 21	Activity 10 – Making Love Decisions
Page 22	Activity 11 – Mutual Compliment
Page 23	Activity 12 – The Mirror Exercise
Page 24	More by Dara Publishing and Strictly Essential Clothing

Copyright © 2017 Dara Wisdom and Empowerment Coaching / Reea Rodney

Standing In Our GReatness
Improving Your Self-Love
Introduction

It is very easy to feel comfortable with ourselves when our accomplishments are acknowledged by a peer, family, or when we get the grades we were hoping for. But what happens if we don't meet our own expectations or the expectations of others? Or, what if something unexpected happens? Often, these unforeseen circumstances can throw us off; we may begin questioning our self-worth and doubting our abilities.

This workbook series was designed as a guide to provide children with the proper tool needed to enhance, improve and develop positive self-esteem traits and practices. Children are introduced to a self-esteem and self-evaluation activities which are created to help them recognize their strength and weakness and provide the foundation for them to build on.

About the Coach / Author
Reea Rodney

Reea Rodney is a wife and mother of three wonderful children who resides in Brooklyn, New York. Originally from Trinidad & Tobago, a small twin island located in the West Indies, she migrated to the United States in 2006 in pursuit of a better life for her family. In addition, Reea is also an Empowerment Life Coach, Children's Author, Motivational Speaker, a Childcare Provider and a Medical Assistant.

Because of her innate passion and desire to help children, Reea was inspired to write children's books via her publishing company, Dara Publishing LLC. She wanted to assist not only the children who were under her care, but children all over the world. Fueled by this purpose, Reea became a Certified Life Coach. The result? Dara Wisdom and Empowerment Coaching. In addition, Reea aspires to be a positive voice of empowerment for children that she herself lacked when she was a child.

She seeks to educate parents and young children through her dynamic mini workshops and self-improvement workbooks. Topics such as Self-Esteem, Self-Love, Self-Celebration, Self-Confidence and Bullying are topics that Reea addresses through her programs. While most of these life skills are not taught in schools they are valuable to a child's overall wellbeing and development.

Standing In Our Greatness

Improving Your Self-Love
What is Self-Love?

Do you feel good about yourself? --- If the answer is yes well... you've already discovered a big secret that some people take a lifetime to know. But if the answer is no or if you aren't sure how you feel, don't worry that's what this workbook is here for.

To make it simple Self-love is loving yourself the best way you can. Self-Love is very important as it determines the way you see yourself, the way you talk about yourself even in your mind and the way you treat others.

When you love yourself, you will do the things that are good and healthy for you like eating your veggies, going to bed on time, doing your homework and being kind to yourself. Practicing Self-Love also makes you feel happy and confident because you are proud of who you are on the inside and outside.

Now that you've learned about Self-Love, do you think you practice Self-Love? If yes list five (5) ways you show yourself love.

1. _____
2. _____
3. _____
4. _____
5. _____

Standing In Our Greatness

Improving Your Self-Love
Why is it Important to Practice Self-Love?

Practicing Self-Love motivates you to take care of yourself in the right way. When you practice Self-Love, it boosts your Self-Esteem and Self-Confidence because you are happy with who you are on the inside and outside. Additionally, practicing Self-Love will further encourage you to work on areas of your life that needs attention so you can be your best healthy and happy self.

Here are a few additional reasons why it is good to practice Self-Love.
- It allows you to project your positive energy;
- It allows you to be the best "you" that you can be;
- It boost your confidence;
- It allows you to love even the part of you that may seem imperfect

Can you give some reason why you think you should practice self-love?

_____
_____
_____

How do you think you can improve your ability to practice Self-Love?

_____
_____
_____

Copyright © 2017 Dara Wisdom and Empowerment Coaching / Reea Rodney

Standing In Our Greatness

Improving Your Self-Love
Positive Impact of Self-Love

As we've discuss earlier, Self-Love is important as it shapes the way we view ourselves and as a result treat ourselves. When you love yourself, and embrace everything about you, there's a tremendous amount of wealth and positive benefit.

Some of the positive benefits of practicing Self-Love are as follows:
- You think positively about yourself;
- You make the right choices e.g. being honest, eating healthy, listening to your parents and teachers etc.;
- You respect yourself and others;
- You will be more assertive and confident;
- You would be motivated to take better care of yourself.

Now that you've learn about some positive impact Self-Love can have on you, can you think of five (5) ways you can benefit from loving yourself?

1 _____
2 _____
3 _____
4 _____
5 _____

Standing In Our Greatness
Improving Your Self-Love
Fun Ways to Promote Self-Love at Home and School

Here are some fun ways to promote self-love at home or at school:

Find something you are good at (i.e. a hobby, sport, game) and spend time doing it at home or school. This will boost you as it would make you happy.

No more comparison. Stop comparing yourself to a friend at school or your sibling at home.

Create a self-ritual that you can do each morning before going to school or at night before bed. For example, say the "I Love Me" affirmation each day.

Celebrate your wins no matter how big or small. Pat yourself on the back and be proud of what you have achieved.

Now that you've learn about some positive impact Self-Love can have on you, can you think of five (5) ways you can benefit from loving yourself?

 _____

  _____

  _____

  _____

5 _____

Standing In Our Greatness
Improving Your Self-Love
Parents Tips for Promoting Self-Love

Connect often: The best way to teach your child about self-love is to communicate with them often, have age appropriate dialogues with them about taking care of themselves, loving themselves, embracing who they are, etc. And when they get to a certain age, be intentional about teaching them what self-love is.

Be open-minded: Create an opening where your kids can come to you and share with you the things that are going on in their lives and the things that may be bothering them, whether at school, home, or with a friend etc. This will be your opportunity to re-enforce all the things you are trying to teach them.

Be the parent, but also a friend: Get to know your child. What do they like to do? What are their talents? Who are their friends and what are their names? What did they do at school today? What are their insecurities? Knowing these things will help to guide you on the things you need to teach them.

Understand your impact: As a parent, you have the power to build your child up or pull them down with the words you speak. Please be aware of what you are saying to your child and how you are speaking to them. Once spoken, words are always the hardest to take back.

Standing In Our GREATNESS
Improving Your Self-Love
More Parents Tips for Promoting Self-Love

Be a role model for your child: Your kids are watching your every move, and they will emulate exactly what they see you do or say. If you are not honoring and respecting yourself, then you are setting the wrong example for your kids.

Focus on what matters: Self-love has less to do with how you look or how you dress yourself. It has more to do with how you respect yourself. Your children know that they are not special because of materialistic things or external things that could be taken away in an instance. They're awesome because of who they are from the inside; let them appreciate that.

Be transparent through your story: Share the good and the bad with your children. Discuss the things that you struggled with, how you overcame them or what you would do differently.

And finally, teach them about joy: Happiness can be taken away… it's external. But joy, that's something that they should have on the inside. And when they leave the house and encounter all of those things in the world that are designed to tear them apart, they'll still have their God-given joy.

Activity 1
Daily Self-Love Worksheet

Keep in touch with how you are feeling on a daily basis.

Date Today:

I LOVE myself today because:

_____

_____

Today I FORGIVE myself because:

_____

_____

I am _____ because: _____

Something GOOD I did for myself was:

_____

_____

Notes:

_____

_____

Activity 2
Support System

A part of practicing self-love is having a self-care support system set in place. This support system can assist you when you need help or guidance. Knowing who you can rely on can make a big difference when you're feeling lost or sad.
Who can I call when...

I am feeling sad and lonely?

I need someone to talk to?

I need help making the right decision?

I need reminding of how special I am?

Activity 3
I Know Who I Am

It's important that you believe in yourself and speak positive about yourself.

- I Am ____
- I Am Unique
- I Am Creative
- I Am Grateful
- I Am Blessed
- I Am ____
- I Am Lovable
- I Am ____
- I Am Abundant
- I Am Joyful
- I AM
- I Am ____
- I Am Talented

Activity 4
Positive Self-Talk Flowers

Directions: Sometimes the negative thoughts we have can make us feel very badly about ourselves. Cross out all the negative thoughts that makes you feel sad or frustrated and color the positive thoughts.

- I can't do it.
- I don't have to be perfect!
- I'm stupid.
- This is hard! I think I can do it.
- I'm a great friend.
- I never do anything right!
- I'll try my best.
- I'll never finish!
- It's OK when things don't go my way. That's life!
- That's not fair!
- I give up!
- I'm in control of my feelings.
- No one's perfect and that's OK!
- This is impossible!
- No one cares about me.
- I can change my thoughts!
- Everyone's better than me.
- Challenges can be good.
- I am loved.
- I can ask for help.

Copyright © 2017 Dara Wisdom and Empowerment Coaching / Reea Rodney

Activity 5
22 Things I Love

This activity would allow a child to identify the things that makes them happy. Each day have your child write down what made them happy on that day. Or they can list all the things they love such as names of food, places, people, things, TV shows, animals, etc.

Activity 6
Making Choices

Making the right choice is a huge part of being responsible and promoting self-love. This activity is designed to help you identify some good and bad choices, so that you can make better decisions while in school, home or with your peers.

Write the choices from below in the list they belong to. Cross the choice off the list once you have used it.

Good Choice	Bad Choice

Hitting / Helping / Hurting People / bullying / Talking Mean

Playing with Friends / Hugging / Being Kind

Saying Bad Words / Sharing

Activity 7
10 Things I Like About Myself

Fill in the blanks and write 10 Things I Like About Myself.

1. _____
2. _____
3. _____
4. _____
5. _____
6. _____
7. _____
8. _____
9. _____
10. _____

Activity 8
My "I Love Me" Jar

Create a label called "I Love Me" and stick it on a jar or box with a lid. On a piece of paper write out affirmations and simple activities promoting self-love (you can even cut it into a heart shape.) Each day have your child take one out. If they can read, have them read it aloud; if they can't, read it to them. This can be an activity they can do daily to promote loving and caring for themselves or things that they love about themselves.

Activity 9
My Comparison Self-Portrait

You're sure to have a blast as you come up with comparisons for your eyes, ears, nose etc.

My hair is _____ like _____

My eyes are _____ as _____

My nose is _____ like _____

My mouth is _____ like _____

My face is _____ as _____

My body is _____ like _____

My hands are _____ like _____

Picture of you:

Activity 10
Making Love Decisions

Practice making loving decisions. Our daily life choices mirror's the amount of care and love we have for ourselves. Use two important questions in your decision making: "Is this (behavior, thought pattern, or friendship) the most loving to me?" and "What are the most loving things I can do for myself (or for others) when a situation arise?"

Make a note of the Love Decisions you've made below. You can do this activity as many times as you want.

My Choices .... My Future

3 good decisions I would like to make this week are:

1 _____

2 _____

3 _____

I predict my future to look like this if I make these choices:

_____
_____
_____
_____
_____

Copyright © 2017 Dara Wisdom and Empowerment Coaching / Reea Rodney

Activity 11
My Positive Self-Image Chart

This activity will help identify your strengths and the things you enjoy or feel good about.

My Positivity Chart

My Name:

Things I am good at:

Things I enjoy:

People I like:

My favorite things:

Picture of me:

What makes me HAPPY:

Activity 12
The Mirror Exercise

The mirror exercise is one of the best exercises that you can do with your child to help them promote Self-Love. It is a simple but very powerful Self-Esteem and Self-Love building activity.

Encourage your child to do this exercise every day for 30 days, and it will change your child's life.

Choose a time in the morning or night and find a quiet place. Look directly into your eyes in the mirror for 2 mins. As you look directly into your eyes say some good and encouraging words to yourself. For example, I am beautiful; I am strong; I am happy; I am amazing, etc. At the end say, "I love You."

The more you do it, the more you'll accept yourself for who you are and feel better about yourself. Eventually you will develop a healthy love for yourself.

Want more great reading?
Check out these books in our series!

Juniper and Rose

"Check out our Dara Publishing Store at www.darapublishingstore.co for our children's books, clothing, and much more."

Strictly Essentials Styles by DARA

Visit our website for more: https:www.darapublishing.co/strictly-essentials/

Dara Wisdom and Empowerment Coaching

www.ingramcontent.com/pod-product-compliance
Lightning Source LLC
LaVergne TN
LVHW072103070426
835508LV00002B/248

9780999750599 3